IMAGES
of America

SCOTCH PLAINS
AND
FANWOOD

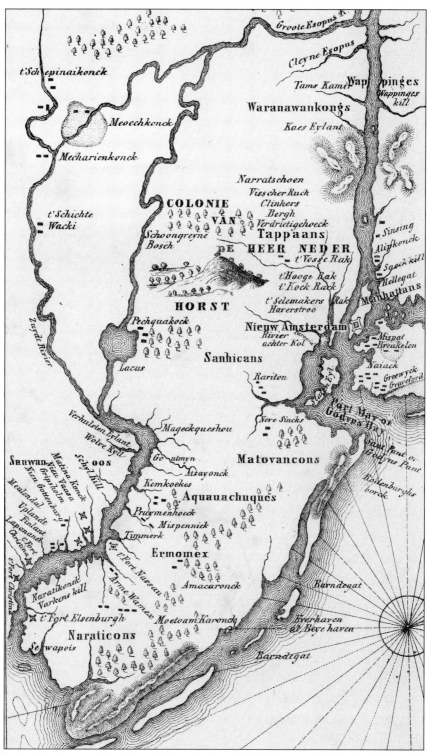

The Vanderdonck map of the New Netherlands, 1656. This map was the foundation of Ogilby's map of 1671 and others published subsequently.

IMAGES
of America

SCOTCH PLAINS
AND
FANWOOD

Richard and Suzanne Bousquet

ARCADIA

First published 1995
Copyright © Richard and Suzanne Bousquet, 1995

ISBN 0-7524-0235-8

Published by Arcadia Publishing,
an imprint of the Chalford Publishing Corporation
One Washington Center, Dover, New Hampshire 03820
Printed in Great Britain

Library of Congress Cataloging-in-Publication Data applied for

We lovingly dedicate this compilation to our daughter, Danielle.
We hope she will cherish our history as we cherish her.

Contents

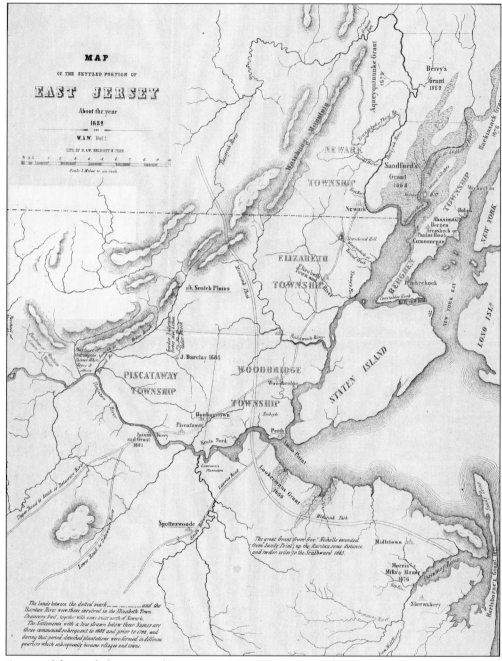

A map of the settled portion of East Jersey, 1682. "It was compiled from various sources and will give the reader an idea of the extent of the settled portion of the province about the time it passed into the possession of the 'twenty-four' [original settlers of this region]." This map was reproduced in 1846 in the collections of the New Jersey Historical Society.

Introduction

Imagine it is the year 1684. You have been at sea for months. You finally come on shore, to find ". . . a land well-settled with people." You begin a journey inland passing droves of deer, elk, wild turkey, beaver, wolves, bears, and rattlesnakes. You encounter a tiny flea—"a troublesome little flea." (Today, we still encounter this troublesome little flea, but we call it a mosquito.)

You continue your journey until you reach the first range of mountains—the "blew hills" of the Watchung Mountains. There, you find mountain streams of fresh water and land for cattle to graze. You walk through fields of wild strawberries so thick you only see the color red. Wood for building abounds in the area. There are no "lawyers, physicians or parsons"—an advantage for those who wish to stake claim to vast tracts of land. You settle here, just "11 miles from New Perth (now Perth Amboy), and 12 miles from Elizabeth-town." Civilization is close, yet not too close.

Our journey begins with this image of the land as it was in the 1600s, and will continue with photographic images of Scotch Plains and Fanwood. Along the way, a unique, privately-owned collection of historic maps will illustrate the increasing development of these areas. This journey will excite the imagination, because our communities have often played an important part in the development of our country. The long and fascinating history of Scotch Plains and Fanwood includes: the acquisition of landrights from the Native Americans in the treaties of 1778 to 1883; the importance of the area for agriculture and transportation via the "Swift Sure stage line" from New York to Philadelphia via Scotch Plains; the Revolutionary War and the Battle of the Short Hills, which was fought in the ash swamp of Scotch Plains in June 1777; the Civil War and evidence of our citizens' involvement in the Underground Railroad; the patriotic loyalty to our country's ideals through times of war and peace . . . Our images capture some moments of these periods, and will preserve these historic moments for our future and our children's future.

Acknowledgments

We would like to thank the Townships of Scotch Plains and Fanwood for their commitment to the Historical Society and the Osborn-Cannonball House museum. We are deeply indebted to the Historical Society of Scotch Plains and Fanwood which permitted us access to their extensive collection of photographs and memorabilia. Every effort was made to retain accuracy in describing the images. We hope that this compilation will serve as a permanent record of the Historical Society's devotion to our local history. Of course, the photographs have been donated to the Historical Society by many individuals and families; we thank those who had the foresight to donate these historical images for future generations.

One
The Way It Was

Farm pastures. This picture is of the Giles farm in Scotch Plains looking toward the Watchung Mountains. The dirt road in the foreground is Mountain Avenue, and in the distance Route 22 would eventually parallel this road. These pastures have long been developed with highways, houses, and businesses.

"A Mapp of New Jersey in America" by John Seller and William Fisher (London, 1677; engraved, colored, 42.5-by-92.2 cm, in 3 sections). The map was a device used to attract potential settlers and investors in the "New-Caeserea or New-Jersey" colony. Notice the

illustrations of Native American life in the 1600s. Also, note the original orientation of the map, with north pointing to the right—the way a ship would encounter land after sailing across the Atlantic.

The rolling hills provided fertile pastures. A careful inspection of the background reveals a large, castle-like home.

A milk factory in Scotch Plains. Raising cows was part of everyday life in the area until the later part of the twentieth century.

A milk wagon (*c*. 1900). Gert Smalley is shown here on the milk run at Bornman's (or Dog Corners) in Scotch Plains.

The home and garden of John Bornman, a carpenter and builder in Scotch Plains (*c*. 1900). The home was located on Westfield Road next to the current Scotch Plains-Fanwood High School. Notice the residents on the front porch.

Another view of John Bornman's home and entrance (*c.* 1898).

The front parlor of the Bornman home at 609 Westfield Road in Scotch Plains. This *c.* 1898 view shows what a typical parlor looked like in rural Union County early in the twentieth century. Notice the foot-pumped organ, globe oil lamp, and horsehair furniture.

The Bornmans (*c.* 1900). John, Mary, and Laude are featured here.

Bornman ancestors (*c.* 1900). These hand-drawn portraits were displayed in the parlor to be photographed for posterity.

The old swimming hole, looking east. This winding creek provided recreation as well as vital resources to local farms. The swimming hole, located on Johnson's farm, is no longer present.

Beneath a dam (1907). This dam was located on the Simeon Lambert farm on Raritan Road in Scotch Plains. Lambert used the dammed water to help run his cider mill and distillery. Of course, others dammed and diverted the natural creeks in the area for grist mills, etc.

Mollenhammer's grounds in Scotch Plains, from *Gems of Plainfield and Vicinity* (published by G. Thorn, Plainfield, N.J.). This stereo-image shows some of the picturesque scenery created by the dams and footbridges in Scotch Plains.

Cider mill (1907). This view is of Simeon Lambert's cider house and distillery on Raritan Road in Scotch Plains.

Simeon Lambert's home, with the old Lambert mill in the background, c. 1907. Located on Raritan Road near Lake Avenue, this photograph depicts the store, home, and barn of Simeon Lambert. The old part of the house was built in 1777; the new part, shown in this photograph, was built between 1844 and 1847. The store served as a social center for the surrounding county for many miles from around 1775 to 1855, but burned in 1914. The property was in the Lambert family until 1908. Lake Avenue was called Quaker Road at the time of this photograph.

Pastoral life in the 1880s.

"Vail of desolation" from *Gems of Plainfield and Vicinity* (published by G. Thorn, Plainfield, N.J.). Double photographs for use in stereoscopes were popular during Victorian times. The view in this stereo-image is of Feltville, which was part of Scotch Plains in the Watchung Mountains.

"Devil's chimney," from *Stereo Gems of New Jersey* (published by G. Thorn, Plainfield, N.J.). Viewing this stereo-image through a stereoscope would make the ravine three-dimensional. Notice the figure on the cliff's edge overlooking the fields of the area.

"The unbroken path." An early road on private land in Scotch Plains. This private road belonged to John Marsh. Notice the bridge and triangular wooden arch at the center of the photograph.

The path to Scotch Plains. This photograph is another view of the unbroken path.

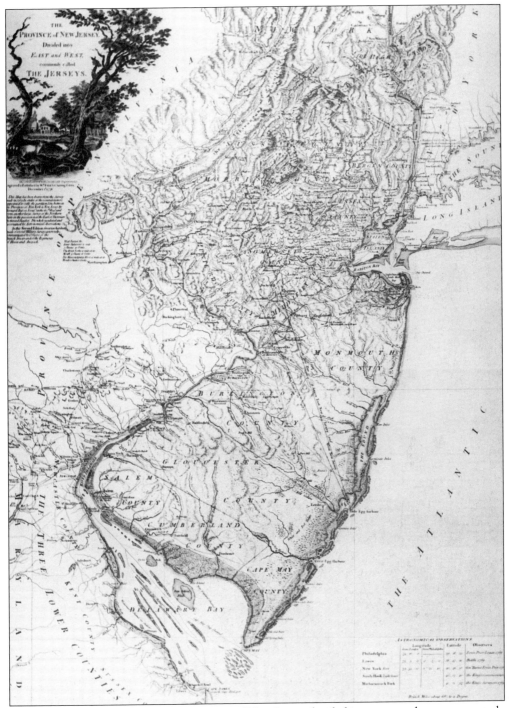

A reproduction of a map of "The province of New Jersey divided into east and west, commonly called the Jerseys." This is from the second edition, "with considerable improvements," engraved and published by Wm. Faden, Charing Cross, December 1, 1778. The map was drawn from the survey made in 1769, and reproduced from the original in the collections of the New Jersey Historical Society, 1976. Scotch Plains appears as Scotsplain.

The famous Terry well, located near the corner of Cooper and Rahway Roads. The well is famous through its association with the Battle of the Short Hills, June 26, 1777, when both Continental and British soldiers stopped to quench their thirst on that hot day and drank the well dry, which had never happened before.

The Terry well (c. 1910). Another view of the well, showing the exterior wood structure, with two boys quenching their thirst. According to a member of the Terry family who still resides in Scotch Plains, the two boys are thought to be Elmer L. Terry (father of Peter Terry) and his brother, Herbert L. Terry, who died in World War I.

William H. Terry was Chairman of the Township Committee from 1895 to 1896.

The Betsy Frazee house as photographed in 1889. Built in the early 1700s in Scotch Plains, the house and its original owner were made famous when Lord Cornwallis of the British army smelled the aroma of fresh-baked bread on his march in 1777. After requesting bread for his men, Betsy Frazee is said to have replied, "I give this, sir, in fear, not in love." The legend holds that Cornwallis then refused the bread by saying, "Then, neither I nor a soldier of mine shall eat it, Madam." All that day, the British troops passed her home but did not disturb her or ask her for a single loaf of bread. The house still stands at the corner of Rahway and Raritan Roads. Note the beehive oven on the right side of the house.

The Betsy Frazee house (c. 1920). This more recent image depicts architectural advances in the structure.

The Betsy Frazee house (c. 1950). A sign on Rahway Road is visible in this photograph. Also note that the beehive oven is still part of the home.

The Thirteen Star house. It was built approximately 1760, originally owned by John Ryno, and subsequently owned by Sea Captain Brown.

The DeCamp burial ground. Located on the corner of Lamberts Mill Road and Buttonwood Lane in Scotch Plains, this family cemetery contains gravestones dating back to 1782. The graves consist of Mr. John DeCamp (d. 1782); Deborah DeCamp (d. 1793), widow of John; Dr. Gideon DeCamp (d. 1815); Freelove DeCamp (d. 1784), daughter of John DeCamp and sister of Dr. Gideon DeCamp; and Sergeant Morris DeCamp, a Revolutionary War veteran serving with the Sheldon's Light Dragoons. The cemetery still exists today on private property, although it cannot be seen from the street.

The Baptist cemetery first known as "God's little acre." The cemetery is located on the corner of Park and Mountain Avenues in Scotch Plains. It is the final resting place of many original settlers and twenty-four soldiers of the Revolutionary War. Notice the early brown sandstone markers. The stone for these markers was quarried in the nearby Watchung Mountains. The Baptist church can be seen in the distance.

A picture of a tombstone dated 1789 from "God's little acre." In fact, the earliest readable tombstone is dated 1758, and marks the grave of Sarah Frazee. However, there are older, more weathered markers in the cemetery dating back to 1742. William Darby, who owned the property, is buried close to the church. There are slaves buried here as well. One was David Allen Drake, who was born a slave and died a free man. Another was "Caesar, an African," who died February 7, 1806, at the age of 104 years. He was a church member for more than fifty years and served as a drover during the Revolution. He was freed after the war. Another distinguished historical figure, Noah Clark, brother of Abraham (a signer of the Declaration of Independence), is buried here.

The Baptist Parsonage house, located at 347 Park Avenue, across from the Scotch Plains Baptist Church on the corner of Park Avenue and Grand Street. On the Grand Street side, by the second-story window, there is a diamond-shaped sandstone bearing the date of construction (1786), making it the first stone parsonage of the then Essex County. This building is on the state and national registers of historical places. It is still standing on its original site. It has a long tradition—it has been the home for every pastor who served the church from 1786 to the present.

The Baptist Parsonage house showing the 1810 wood frame addition on the right side.

Another view of the Baptist Parsonage house. Notice the masonry detail in the chimneys which reveals the construction during two different eras.

The Second Baptist Church at 1964 Grand Street in Scotch Plains. Now known as the Northside YMCA, this building served as the Second Baptist Church after the original meeting house burned to the ground during the winter of 1816–17. This "old meeting house" was built at a cost of $2,492 and was moved to its present location on Grand Street in 1871 with many yokes of oxen. It was then opened as the District 14 School and continued in that service until 1890, when School One was opened. This building then served both church and community until 1910, when Dr. J. Ackerman Coles and his sister Emile purchased the building. In 1912 the "parish house," as it was then called, was opened with a new gymnasium, bowling alleys, and a columned facade. It continues to serve the community as a day care center and gymnasium for the YMCA.

The Scotch Plains Baptist Church at 333 Park Avenue in Scotch Plains. This is the third Baptist church erected on this site. It was built in 1870 at the cost of $23,000. The first service was held in 1871. It is one of the few Victorian gothic churches built in Union County. The original structure is "110 feet in length and made of pressed brick with Ohio stone and white brick trimmings, . . . and transept corner tower and spire 120 feet in height." Notice the surrounding undeveloped property.

A later view of the Scotch Plains Baptist Church. The trees have grown, a wrought iron fence has been added, and power lines and street lights are visible. What cannot be seen in this picture is the 1958 Christian Education building addition to the rear of the church, which was added at the cost of $30,000.

The Osborn-Cannonball House. This structure was built in the mid-1700s, with a fieldstone foundation and wide weather clapboard. The house stands in its original setting, and was occupied as a single-family home until 1972. It is owned by the Township of Scotch Plains and is the home of the Historical Society of Scotch Plains and Fanwood. It has been partially restored to its original structure, including an authentic hand-split wood shingle roof, beehive oven, and colonial kitchen. The parlor retains its Victorian decor to show the changes through the years. The garden is a recreated eighteenth-century working herb garden; it has been featured in many national publications, and was recently featured by the Smithsonian Institute of Washington, D.C. Local sources report that during the Revolutionary War a cannonball landed in the side of this house during a skirmish between British troops and the Patriots.

The Osborn-Cannonball House undergoing an exterior renovation by the Historical Society of Scotch Plains and Fanwood. The renovation was designed to recapture the home's original colonial appearance; notice, for example, the front porch has been decreased in size.

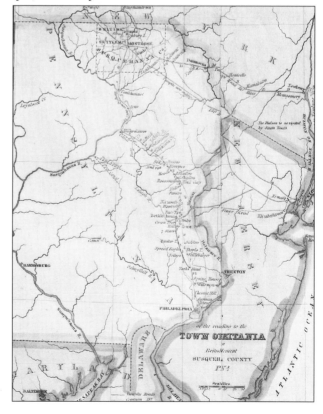

A c. 1819 map of the "roading" to the town of Britania (in Pennsylvania), a British settlement. The map has been damaged, and its repair causes the title "Town of Britania" to read erroneously as "Town Oritania." Notice the stage roads from New York via Newark, Elizabethtown (now Elizabeth), and Easton leading to Philadelphia.

The W.L. Deegans Hotel at 366 Park Avenue in Scotch Plains. Originally built and opened as an inn in 1737 by John Sutton, it has been known as Ye Olde Historical Inn, the Stanbury Inn, Ye Olde Tavern, Sutton's Tavern, and De Boud's Hotel, but has most recently been known as the Stage House Inn. The history of the site dates back prior to white settlers—during excavation for restoration the remains of a Lene Lenape village was uncovered on these grounds. In fact, quantities of oyster and clam shells were unearthed, proving that these seafood-loving Native Americans camped on this site over long periods of time. The inn became the focal point of local activity, serving not only as a restaurant and inn but also as a post office and political meeting place. Its location on the old York Road (which ran from Elizabethtown to Lambertsville) insured the building's introduction to the commercial world as stage lines reached out between New York and Philadelphia. Sutton's Tavern became a regular port of call on the Swift Sure stage line. During the Revolutionary War, the inn was the chief meeting place for troop messengers and officers. Lafayette and his aids stopped at the hotel when General Washington was encamped nearby. The owner at that time was Colonel Recompense Stanbury II, who had joined Jedidiah Swan's company of local men after he had already been wounded in the Battle of Long Island. During the Civil War, there were rallies here as President Lincoln called up more troops in defense of the Union. This postcard shows the local inn as it appeared in the 1880s.

Ye Olde Historic Inn: a later view (c. 1898). The road in the foreground is Front Street in Scotch Plains. Notice the spire of the Scotch Plains Baptist Church behind the left section of the building.

The Old Tavern, Scotch Plains, New Jersey. Another antique postcard. Notice the sign pointing to Plainfield on Front Street.

The home of Colonel Recompense Stanbury II (one of the first proprietors of Ye Olde Historic Inn) and his son, William C. Stanbury. William is sitting on the front porch in this picture.

A photograph of William C. Stanbury, son of Colonel Recompense Stanbury II.

Captain William Piatt's home was built approximately 1740 and demolished in 1954. The home stood at 1805 Front Street in Scotch Plains. Captain Piatt was killed fighting Native Americans at Fort Recovery, Ohio, in Saint Clair's Defeat. Captain Piatt was one of General Washington's personal bodyguards, and his son, William the II, welcomed and entertained General Lafayette on his second visit to this country. Legend has it that this home also was hit with a cannonball during skirmishes between the British and the Patriots.

Another view of Captain Piatt's home with vintage transportation.

The Frazee Lee house presently located at 11 Black Birch Road, Scotch Plains. In fact, the house is made up of two historic homes joined together in 1828. The home includes two additions, one in 1950 and one in 1963. The larger, older section was built by Thomas Lee Senior and has been moved twice. It was originally located on the northeast corner of Cooper and Terrill Roads, and was moved by Samuel Lee in 1828 and joined to a smaller section built by Moses Frazee. It stood for two hundred years on the present Union County Vocational Technical School grounds. It was moved to its present location on Black Birch Road in 1963 when its second addition was built.

The home of William Stillger, located at 1818 Front Street in Scotch Plains. William was a bootmaker, and the grandfather of Marion Clark, who later resided here.

36

The Johnson homestead (*c.* 1890).

Local residents (*c.* 1890).

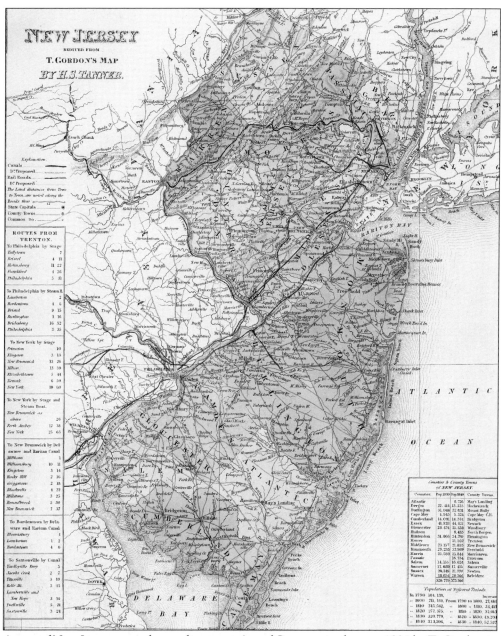

A map of New Jersey entered according to an Act of Congress in the year 1834 by T. Gordon in the Clerk's Office of the District Court of New Jersey. The map locates Scotch Plains in Essex County. Notice that Union County did not exist at the time. Also note the charts on the left, which show various routes by stage and steamboat. In the right lower corner, the population is given by county and decade. For instance, the population of Essex County in 1840 was 44,621. The entire population of New Jersey in 1840 was 373,306—an increase of 52,527 from 1830.

Two

The Blue Hills

"Through the gorge" from *Views of Scotch Plains, Fanwood, and Feltville, New Jersey* (photographed and published by G. Thorn of Plainfield, New Jersey, *c.* 1880). The gorge presented a natural access to the mountain region. The view in this stereo-image may depict an early version of Diamond Hill Road—the road between Scotch Plains and Berkeley Heights.

The mill in Feltville (the Deserted Village), located about a mile north of the town of Scotch Plains in the Watchung Mountains. According to *Views of Scotch Plains, Fanwood and Feltville, New Jersey*, "It is noted for a rift in the mountainside known as the cataract from whose rocky wall gushes a spring of pure, cold water. It has long been a favorite spot for picnic and party." Legend has it that the site was discovered by Native Americans and was known for its supply of pure water. A village was developed by David Felt to house the employees of his paper mills in the 1840s. By 1845 there were thirty-five houses, a church, and a school. The business ultimately failed around the Civil War: the mills closed, and the employees abandoned the village. Later purchased by an entrepreneur from New York, the village failed again and was again deserted. Eventually, the village changed hands again; this time it was purchased by Warren Ackerman, a Scotch Plains business man, who intended to create a vacation retreat, but Feltville's destiny was the same. It has come to be called the Deserted Village and is now owned by Union County and is currently undergoing major restoration.

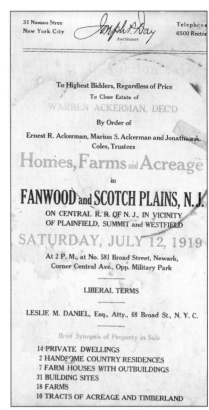

An advertisement for the sale of homes, farms, and acreage in Fanwood and Scotch Plains on July 12, 1919, by the estate of Warren Ackerman. The auction consisted of about 80 parcels of land and included the area of Feltville (today known as Glenside Park).

Another old mill located at the base of the gorge. This mill, as well as the others, utilized the water of the Green Brook for power. This building still stands today near the corner of Diamond Hill Road and Bonnie Burn Road.

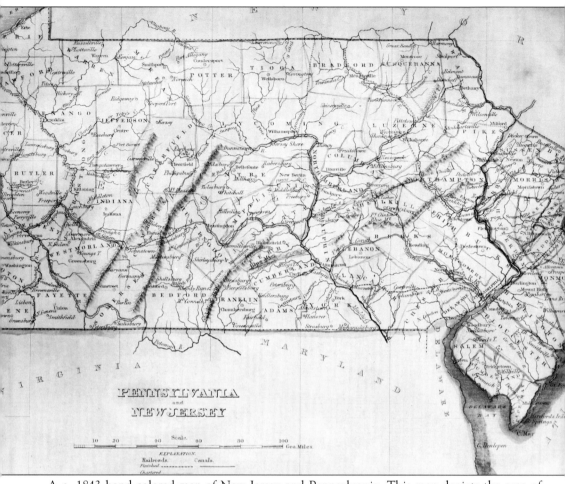

A *c.* 1843 hand-colored map of New Jersey and Pennsylvania. This map depicts the area of Scotch Plains as part of Essex County. Also notice that Scotch Plains does not appear on the map—an indication that despite the local mills and businesses, Scotch Plains was not yet a major player in the state, still retaining its small-town flavor.

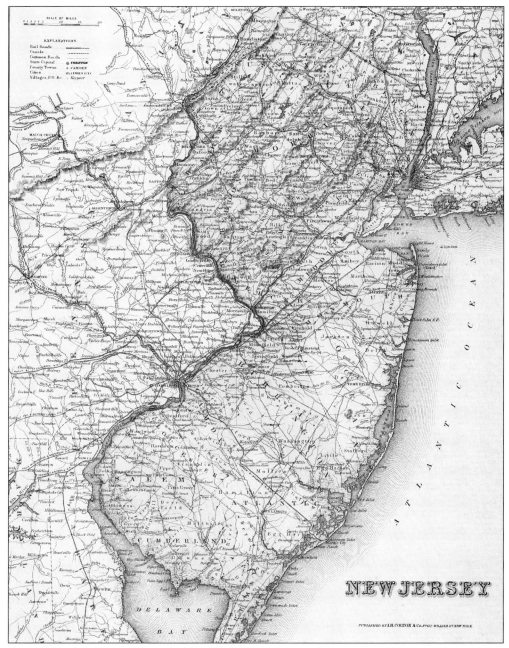

An 1855 map of New Jersey, published by J.H. Colton and Company of William Street, New York. It was #172, entered according to an Act of Congress in 1855 in the Clerk's Office of the District Court for the Southern District of New York. On this map, Scotch Plains is situated on the Jersey Central Railroad from Elizabeth to Clinton. The map is hand-colored and identifies the counties; Scotch Plains remains part of Essex County. Notice that although Fanwood is not yet indicated on the map, Feltville is depicted in the Watchung Mountains. (Map courtesy of the McManus family of Scotch Plains)

Edmund A. Seeley in the late 1800s (photographed by Guillermo Thorn of Plainfield, NJ). Seeley was a prominent Scotch Plains businessman who founded a mill in the Watchung Mountains utilizing the Green Brook for power.

The home of Edmund A. Seeley. This Victorian home was situated in the mountains above Seeley's Pond. In this view, the entire front of the house is visible. The house has been demolished, and the property belongs to Union County Parks System.

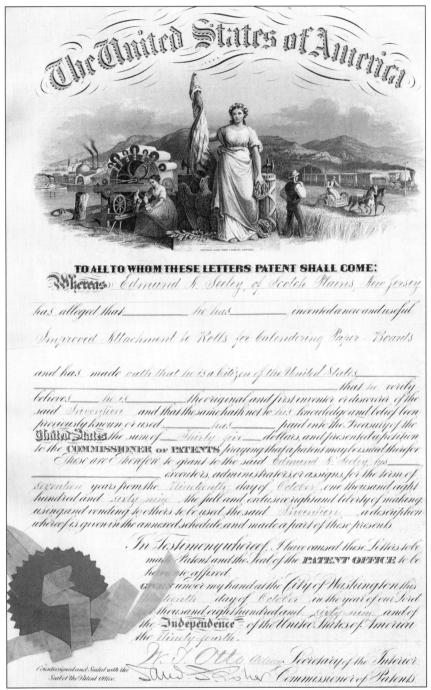

A patent of Edmund A. Seeley. Edmund A. Seeley owned several U.S. patents. The one reproduced here from October 19, 1869, included a drawing for an improvement to the rolling process in the production of paper. Other similar patents obtained by Seeley are in the possession of the Historical Society of Scotch Plains and Fanwood.

Another view of Seeley's home. In this photograph, the waterfalls can be seen.

Seeley's home is in the background of this photograph. The woman on the right was Marian Goodwin.

Florence Allen (*c.* 1900), the niece of Edmund A. Seeley. She lived in his home with her sisters, Frances and Clara Allen, and her aunt Emma Seeley, sister of Edmund. History refers to them all as maiden ladies.

A *c.* 1919 photograph of, from left to right, Emma Seeley, Frances Allen, Dorothy Seeley Osland, and Florence Allen.

Exploring the Green Brook below Seeley's Pond.

The old bridge and ice house. Residents can be seen standing on the bridge in this view of Seeley's bridge and ice house, at the junction of Green Brook and Blue Brook below the dam forming Seeley's Pond.

Seeley's paper mills from *Views in Scotch Plains, Fanwood and Feltville, New Jersey*. The stereo-image caption reads: "These mills are charmingly situated centred of the gorge, a site both wild and romantic. Long known as the Fall Mill—a grist mill having been established here 120 years ago." The description of Scotch Plains from the stereo-image caption is written to entice potential residents: "Scotch Plains, New Jersey is pleasantly situated at the foot of the first mountain, two miles east of Plainfield. It derived its name from Scotch immigrants in 1684. The soil is fertile; a nearly level plain, bounded by the mountains on the north, while hills of gentle undulating lines rise to the south. Nature has been munificent in charming scenery. Green Brook, a sylvan stream of no slight importance, breaks through a delightful gorge, leaping rocky barriers in silvery cascades, forming miniature lakes, mirroring the great rocks and vernal green of the mountain in entrancing beauty. There are also private parks, where art has assisted nature, combining in harmonious effects beauties rarely excelled. Scotch Plains has three churches, a comfortable public school building, paper and fur mills, and a number of stores, hotel, &c."

A *c.* 1900 view of Seeley's Mill. Close inspection reveals a worker in a second-floor window of the mill.

This picture of the mill was taken in July 1916, and indicates the wrath of the Green Brook. (Notice the second-floor addition with overhang and braces is absent in the preceding picture.)

"Sandwiched—a glimpse of the old and the new" from *Artistic Photo Views, Scotch Plains, Fanwood and Feltville* (Series J, Second Edition; published by G. Thorn, Plainfield, NJ). This stereo-image shows both the new and old buildings of Seeley's mills and the surrounding area.

Cook's crusher, *c.* 1889, north of the gorge on the Green Brook. The steep mountain provided water power for use in quarrying stone.

A more contemporary view of stone crushing in Scotch Plains, *c.* 1950.

The road to the paper mill at Cook's Pond.

The 1908 U.S. Geological Survey of the New Jersey-New York Passaic Quadrangle. Notice the lighter areas running from North Plainfield through Summit along the Blue Brook. These mountain areas just northwest of the words, "Scotch Plains," are identified on the map with "RM" and a symbol of crossed hammers. The map legend indicates that these are the mines and quarries for road material. According to the map legend on the right, this lighter area consists of the Triassic formation of igneous rocks (Palisade diabase and Watchung basalt).

The Hollingsworth Fur Mill, *c.* 1890, located just below Seeley's Mill on the Green Brook in the Watchung Mountains. Close inspection reveals many people working. The smoke stack of Seeley's Mill can be seen in the distance in the top right corner.

Getting ready for the hunt at one of the local homes of the Hollingsworth family.

Albert Darby Hollingsworth, *c*. 1900.

"The Christmas hunt, the snow storm," published in 1890 by B.W. Kilburn. Many local residents hunted for deer and other game in the local mountains.

"The hunters, home again," published in 1890 by B.W. Kilburn.

Sleigh riding in the mountains. Laura Bell Moffett Goodwin is fourth from the left in this photograph.

Three

Mapping Progress

An early 1656 map of New Jersey. Notice the Native American names which we still use today.

An 1864 map of Pennsylvania and New Jersey, published by A.J. Johnson, New York. By an act approved by the New Jersey Legislature on March 19, 1857, a separate county—Union County—was formed and became effective on April 13, 1857. This map includes Union

County—the youngest of the twenty-one counties of New Jersey. Scotch Plains does not appear on this map.

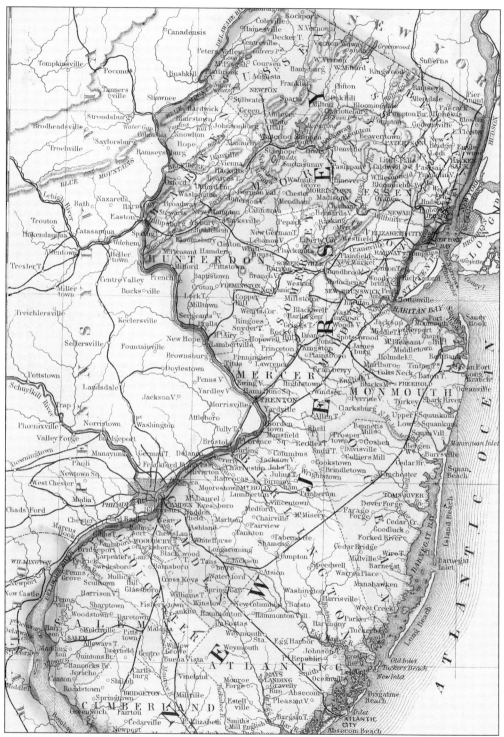

An 1865 county map of New Jersey, drawn and engraved by W.H. Gamble of Philadelphia for S. Augustus Mitchell Jr. Another map of the times showing Union County; again, Scotch Plains is not indicated.

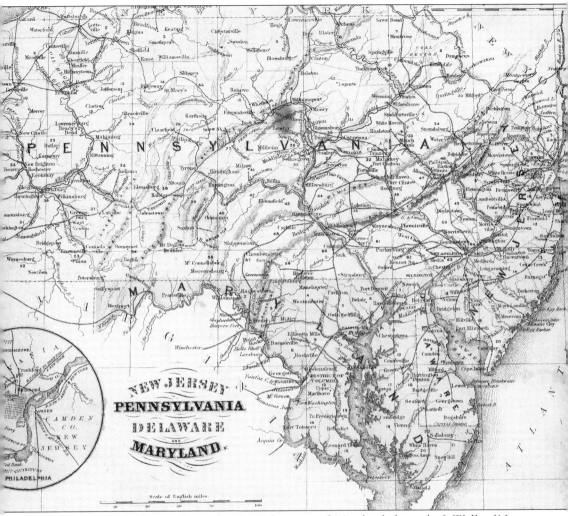

An 1870 map of New Jersey, Pennsylvania, Delaware, and Maryland, drawn by J. Wells of New York. It originally appeared as Map #9 in *McNally's System of Geography*.

An 1872 map of Pennsylvania and New Jersey by Asher and Adams. At long last, Scotch Plains

is included in this more detailed account of New Jersey and its counties.

Fanwood appears for the first time in the 1894 New Business Atlas Map of New Jersey, originally printed by Rand-McNally and Companies in the *Indexed Atlas of the World*. The town name is noted twice: once to locate the town and once for the stop on the Central Railroad line. Scotch Plains is indicated on the map only once.

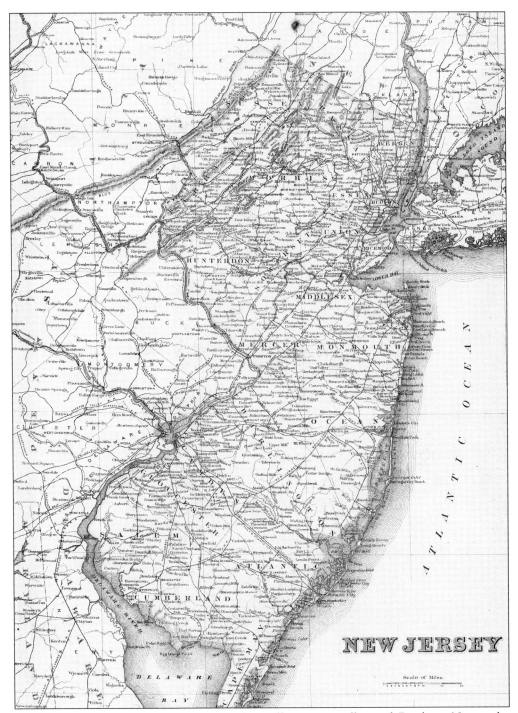

A map of New Jersey published in 1896 by William M. Bradley and Brothers. Notice the inclusion of "Fawnwood Park" (as opposed to Fanwood) as a community located south of Scotch Plains on the Central Railroad of New Jersey.

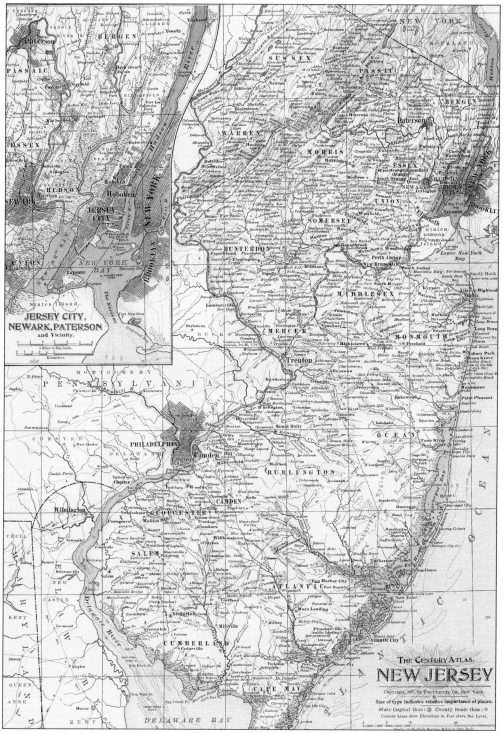

A map from the *Century Atlas of New Jersey*, published in 1897 by the Century Company of New York. The map legend reads "Size of type indicates relative importance of places." In this listing, Scotch Plains reads as one word.

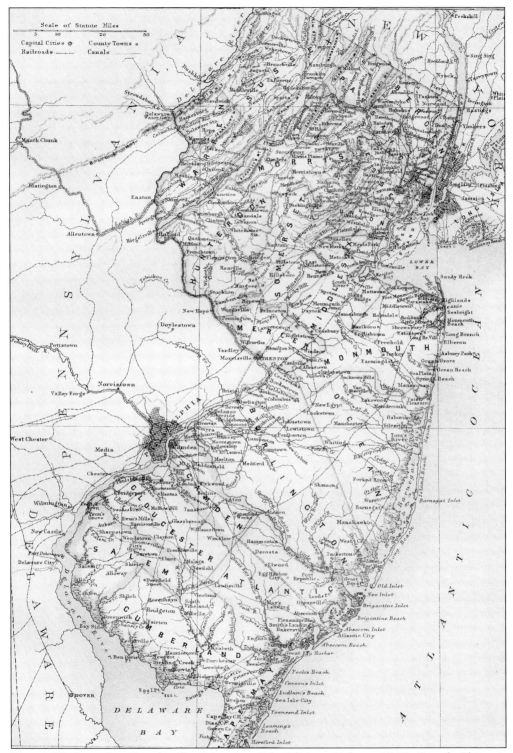

Plate VIII from the *Encyclopedia Britannica*, 9th Edition, Volume XVII. Scotch Plains is indicated; the absence of Fanwood probably dates this map prior to 1894.

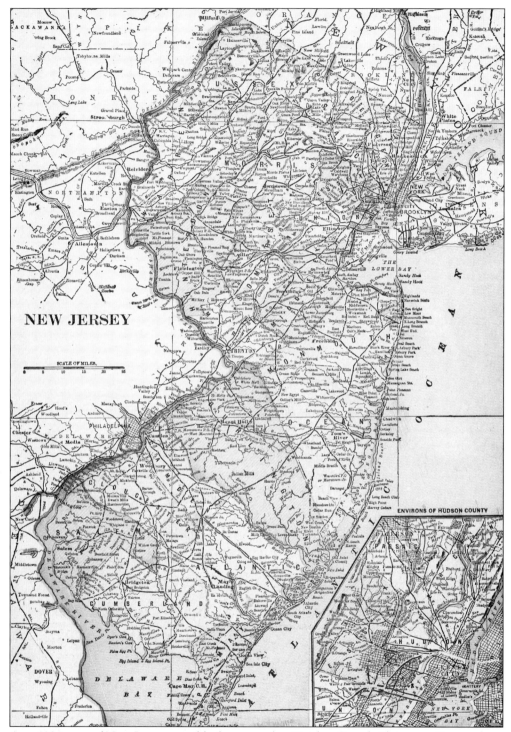

A c. 1904 map of New Jersey, possibly from an atlas. Neither Scotch Plains nor Fanwood are listed as chief cities in the map index.

Four

Fanwood

The Central Railroad station of New Jersey. This postcard from 1875 shows the two-and-a-half-story, stick-style building constructed in 1874 by the Jersey Central Railroad. This building was the second train station in Fanwood.

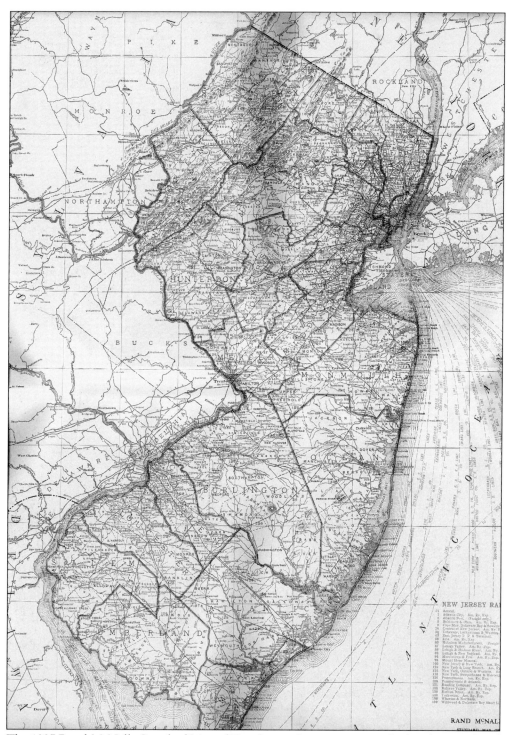

The 1927 Rand-McNally Standard Map of New Jersey, from a commercial atlas, shows railroad and coastal shipping lines. Fanwood and Scotch Plains appear on the map but not in the legend listing principal cities.

The train station at Fanwood today. The building was donated to Fanwood by the Jersey Central Railroad in 1964, and is undergoing historic restoration. The restoration is nearly complete and the station is used frequently by many community groups today.

The pedestrian bridge of the Fanwood train station before the restoration. Notice the train station in the background. This pedestrian walkway has been rebuilt, and it links the eastbound and westbound railroad platforms.

The original building and site of the Fanwood railroad station at Martine and Woodland Avenues. Before 1870, the railroad ran through Fanwood down what is now Midway Avenue.

The Homestead used by Washington as Headquarters. Fanwood, N. J.

A *c.* 1910 photograph of the modernized J.H. Martine home in Fanwood. Originally built in 1774, it was situated at 40–42 Martine Avenue, but is no longer standing. Legend has it that the home was used by General George Washington for his headquarters.

The original pre-Revolutionary War farmhouse that was modernized and became the J.H. Martine home.

The J.H. Martine home during the winter, c. 1920. The piazza and dormers were added around 1900. The building was torn down in the 1930s.

The Fanwood Post Office, c. 1897. This building, the original site of the Fanwood Post Office, was erected in 1897. It served the community as both the post office and library until 1928. During World War II it served as the local Red Cross center. Today, the building still stands on its original site at the corner of Martine and North Avenues.

A c. 1940 photograph of the second Fanwood Library, located on South Avenue in Fanwood.

The second Fanwood Post Office, *c*. 1940. Located on South Avenue in Fanwood, just east of Martine Avenue, this second post office stood across the street from the current one.

The Fanwood oak. This majestic oak tree stands today, shading Martine Avenue in Fanwood. The tree is thought to be the second largest in the state of New Jersey, and it is protected by the Union County Shade Tree Commission. Over the years, tree surgery has helped to preserve this grand old oak. Notice the mixed concrete and asphalt roadway, and the absence of curbing, in this *c*. 1940 photograph.

The Watchung Mountains (Scotch Plains), Fanwood, N.J., c. 1890. Even at the turn of the century, the area retained its rural quality.

Fanwood Township Tax Bill 1883.

Taxes are now due and payable to me **BEFORE** the 20th day of December next. If not paid before that date the delinquent will then be returned to a Justice of the Peace for Prosecution, and 12 per cent. interest and cost will be added.

The Court of Appeals in cases of Taxation will meet at the Truck House of Excelsior H. & L. Co., Scotch Plains, on the Fourth Tuesday in November, at one o'clock, P.M.

Taxes received at B. Connett's on Friday, December 14th, at J. Lambert's Mill on Saturday, December the 15th, from 9 A. M. to 12 M., at the Truck House of Excelsior H. & L. Co., at Scotch Plains, on Monday and Tuesday, Dec. 17th and 18th, and at Chas. A. Smith's Office, near the R. R. Station, on Wednesday, the 19th, from 9 A. M. to 1 P. M.

Taxes received at home on other days previous to the 20th (Sundays excepted).

Payment before the 20th day of December is respectfully requested.

RATE ON $100.00 VALUATION.

County Tax,	- -	52 Cts.
Township Tax,	- -	12 "
State School Tax,	- -	25 "
Road Tax,	-	16 "
Amount Exclusive of Specials,		$1.05

SPECIAL TAXES.

Road District, No. 4,	-	7½ Cts.
School do. do.4,	-	55 do.
do. do. do.11	-	08 do.
do. do. do. 11, (Middlesex Co.)	07½ do.
do. do. do. 14,	-	25 do.

Wm. HETFIELD, Collector.
P. O. Box 1180,   Plainfield, N. J.
If sent by mail, please enclose postage stamp for receipt.
☞ PROMPT PAYMENT IS REQUESTED.
☞ Bring or send your Bills.

Fanwood, N. J., October 1st, 1883.

Mr. *William D. Johnston*

Your Taxes due the Township of Fanwood for the year 1883 are :

Description of Property. *Lot & Barn*

VALUATION—Real Estate,	....	$ *100*
do. Personal,	....	*25*
Total Valuation,	....	$ *125*
Legal Deductions,	.... ..	
Value of Taxable Property,	.....$ *125*	$ Cts.

Poll Tax,	
Dog Tax,	
County Tax,	*65*
Township Tax,	*15*
State School Tax,	*32*
Special School Tax,	*32*
Road Tax,	*20*
Special Road Tax,	

$ *1.64*

Less Road Tax Worked,
Less Deductions by Com. of Appeals, *Certificate*
Less Deductions for Fireman,
Interest,
Costs,

Received Payment, *Dec 20th 1883* AMOUNT, $

Wm. Hetfield ..... *Collector.*

An 1883 Fanwood Township tax bill for Mr. William D. Johnson for one lot and barn. This township tax bill includes real estate tax, personal tax, school tax, and a variety of other assessments. How does this compare with tax bills today?

An Ordinance

TO REGULATE THE USE OF

BICYCLES, TRICYCLES

AND SIMILAR VEHICLES AND OTHER ROAD VEHICLES,

In the Public Roads, Streets and Highways

OF THE

TOWNSHIP OF FANWOOD.

The Inhabitants of the Township of Fanwood by their Township Committee do enact as follows:

Section 1. That all Bicycles, Tricycles and similar vehicles when in use on the public highways, streets or roads within the Township of Fanwood are hereafter required to have a lamp of such illuminating power as to be plainly seen one hundred yards, attached thereto, and kept lighted between one hour after sunset and sunrise.

Sec. 2. That all Bicycles, Tricycles and similar Vehicles shall carry a suitable bell attached to the handle-bar of the machine, which when rung may be heard 100 feet distant. That such bell shall be sounded as an alarm by the rider of such vehicle upon approaching another vehicle from the rear, or upon approaching pedestrians crossing the street, or upon the approach of another vehicle on the same street, or on a street intersecting the street, road or highway riden upon.

Sec. 3. That no person shall ride upon any bicycle, tricycle or similar machine upon any sidewalk within the limits of the township of Fanwood, providing that the term sidewalk as used in this ordinance shall be construed to mean such sidewalk only concerning which the inhabitants of the township of Fanwood have power to pass ordinances under and by virtue of paragraph V. Section 1 Chapter 8, of the Public Laws of 1896, and provided, further that this section shall not apply to the riding of any bicycle, tricycle or similar machine upon any sidewalk when necessary to ride upon said sidewalk in passing to or from private premises to or rom the roadbed of any street, road or highway.

Sec. 4. That no person shall ride upon any BICYCLE, TRICYCLE or SIMILAR VEHICLE, or OTHER ROAD VEHICLE IN ANY PUBLIC ROAD, STREET or HIGHWAY OF THE TOWNSHIP OF FANWOOD AT A GREATER SPEED THAN THE RATE OF TWELVE MILES PER HOUR.

Sec. 5. That every violation of any of the provisions of this ordinance shall render the OFFENDER subject to a fine not exceeding the sum of FIVE DOLLARS FOR EACH OFFENCE, and that the Justice of the Peace or other magistrate who may have jurisdiction over such offences, in violation of this ordinance may impose such fine in his discretion as he may think proper, not exceeding the sum of Five Dollars for each offence.

Adopted July 8, 1897.

EDWARD L. HAND,
Township Clerk.

An 1897 ordinance issued by Edward L. Hand, the township clerk of Fanwood, "To regulate the use of bicycles, tricycles and similar vehicles and other road vehicles in the public roads, streets and highways of the township of Fanwood."

REGULAR

Republican Ticket.

Fanwood Township, Union County, New Jersey,

Election to be held March 8, 1904.

For Chosen Freeholder, (2 years)
JOHN ROBISON.

For Member Township Committee, (3 years)
CHARLES BALL.

For Justice of the Peace, (4 years)

For Constable, (3 years)
ROBERT WARPOLE.

For Overseer of Poor, (3 years)
AUGUST KLEMPSER.

For Commissioner of Appeals, (3 years)
WILLIAM H. JOHNSTON.

For Surveyors of Highways, (1 year)
ANDREW SCHAFFER,
LEWIS B. CODDINGTON.

For Pound Keepers,
HENRY S. LITTELL,
JOHN EDWARDS,
NICHOLAS DELNERO.

APPROPRIATIONS.

Public Roads $2000.00
Sidewalks.... .... $250.00
For Support of Poor $400.00
Police Department.............. $100.00
Fire Department $300.00

The next Township Election to be held at Excelsior Hall, Scotch Plains, N. J.

The Republican Ticket of Fanwood Township, Union County, New Jersey, for the election of March 8, 1904. It should be noted that Scotch Plains and Fanwood operated as one community, referred to as Fanwood Township. Notice the bottom of the flier announcing the next township election to be held at the Excelsior Hall of Scotch Plains. Excelsior Hall was one of the fire houses of the area.

1882.

Fanwood Township.

NATIONAL TICKET.

ANTI-MONOPOLY.

For Representative in Congress—3d District,
BENJAMIN URNER.

[The balance of this Ticket is Republican]

For Member of Assembly—3d District,
FRANK L. SHELDON.
For County Clerk,
WILLIAM CRANSTOUN, JR.
For Surrogate,
GEORGE T. PARROT.
For Coroner.
ISRAEL B. LUKENS.

The 1882 Fanwood Township National Ticket. Politics in 1882 involved "business as usual."

TEMPERANCE PIC-NIC.

GRAND PIC-NIC

OF THE

Scotch Plains Div., No. 139, S. of T.,

TO THE

Washington Springs, Feltville,

Wednesday, Sept. 6, 1871.

TICKETS 25 CENTS.

A "Temperance Pic-nic" invitation dated Wednesday, September 6, 1871, for a picnic at Washington Springs (also known as the Cataract), Feltville, in the Watchung Mountains.

Five
Scotch Plains

"Main Street," Scotch Plains, N.J. This *c.* 1897 postcard depicts the business district between Second and Grand Streets on Park Avenue.

The trolley line from Westfield to Elizabeth, c. 1900. Similar trolleys connected Scotch Plains with Plainfield on Front Street.

Another view of the trolley to Elizabeth from Westfield.

The Paff Hotel, at the corner of Second Street and Park Avenue in Scotch Plains, c. 1900. Notice the street sign pointing to Westfield. The photograph suggests a prosperous business center. The building still exists today—although modernization has completely covered the original structure.

The home of Thomas Paff, c. 1900, with Mr. Paff and family on the front porch. Notice the well immediately to the right of the front stairs—the next best thing to indoor running water.

An 1898 photograph of Paff's grocery store, located on the corner of Park and Bartle Avenues. In front of the store are Charlie Wade and Henry Marsh. Notice the product advertisements in and beneath the window. The fainter sign to the right of the door announces a football game between Scotch Plains and Westfield. This corner now is the site of Russo's Business Machines, Inc. at 393 Park Avenue. (Photograph courtesy of Russo's Business Machines, Inc., Scotch Plains)

John's Meat Market on Park Avenue in 1939. This photograph is of John Losavio in front of his store at 389 Park Avenue. Compare the prices of meat today . . . The site was once the home of the *Union City Herald*. (Photograph courtesy of John's Meat Market, Scotch Plains)

A 1950s view of Park Avenue opposite the Municipal Building.

A *c.* 1900 view of Mountain Avenue (or Springfield Road), looking east. The house on the left was owned by Mrs. Cook, and was where the Moffitts lived. The tree-lined rural beauty of this street is still cherished today.

A c. 1900 photograph of Deerhurst, the Coles estate on Mountain Avenue in Scotch Plains.

Deerhurst was adorned with many bronze statues. Featured in this photograph are Dorothy Eller and Audrey Weekley.

Dorothy Eller and Audrey Weekley posing with more sculptures on the Coles estate.

Besides the sculptures, the grounds of Deerhurst were decorated with beautiful, real wildlife.

Dr. J. Ackerman Coles at Deerhurst.

Local residents in town, c. 1897. From left to right are Fred Smith, Arthur Chapin, Roy Day, and Ernest Marsh (who died at the age of eighteen of consumption).

The Scotch Plains Bucket and Engine Company, or the Chemical Fire Company, in 1911. From left to right are: (front row) Tom O'Keefe, Harry Pangborn, Wm. Jamerson, Rich Hart, Chas. Meyer, Frank Weldon, Wm. Spicer, Henry Meyer (brother of Chas.), and Wm. Nestey; (middle row) Geo. Keuhn, Roy Day, Wm. Gist, Johnny Shiffel, Burt Debby, Fred Schmidt, James Hunter, Wm. Meyer (brother of Chas. and Henry), O. Cecil Reinhart, John Coles (owner of the land that is currently the site of the Scotch Plains Post Office and apartments), James Carrono, Chas. Eller, John Realdan, Alphonse Sabatinio (the town barber), Geo. Johnson (the Union City Sheriff), and Wm. Deegan (owner of the bar at the Stage House Inn); (back row) James Johansen, Lynus Walpole (owner of the saloon on Second Street and Park Avenue where the Paff Hotel was located), Jos. Albert, Wm. Debby, Anthony Albert, Wm. Dingwold (publisher of the *Union City Herald*), and Wm. Buckley. "Rags," the dog in the front row, belonged to George Keuhn. The chief's megaphone and hat are behind the dog; the hat reads Fanwood Township.

The Scotch Plains Bucket and Engine Company, first organized in 1884. The horse is pulling a Holloway chemical engine. The building once housed Meyer Brothers Grocery. From left to right are Henry Meyer (holding the lantern), Jos. Albert, Wm. Meyer, and Chief Chas. Meyer Sr. The two men at the far right remain unidentified.

Proud and on parade! The Cawley Mountain Water Company on parade, *c.* 1900.

Another view of the parade, c. 1900.

The fire fighters of Westfield, c. 1900.

West End fire fighters, c. 1900.

One of the many entertaining aspects of the parade—a concert band.

90

More fire equipment on parade. The words "Red Jacket" appear on the firehose on the first wagon.

Equipment of the Fanwood Fire Department.

The Scotch Plains Rescue Squad building, c. 1950. Previously the home of the Scotch Plains Bucket and Engine Company, the building still stands today (with a newer masonry facade) and is still the home of the Scotch Plains Rescue Squad.

The Scotch Plains Municipal Building, c. 1930, showing fire and rescue equipment.

A close-up of the fire-fighting equipment in front of the municipal building.

A full view of the first Scotch Plains Municipal Building on Park Avenue in Scotch Plains. The ground-breaking ceremony took place in 1927, and the building was completed in 1928.

A postcard view of the Scotch Plains Municipal Building.

A c. 1900 photograph of the house at the corner of Park Avenue and Front Street where the Village Green now stands. Originally owned by John Marsh, it was sold in 1911 to Henry C. Meyer. The building was razed to make way for the new Scotch Plains Municipal Building.

94

Another view, this time from the back, of the house at the corner of Park Avenue and Front Street.

John Marsh was Chairman of the Township Committee from 1879 to 1882, and 1884.

An earlier tin-type photograph of John Marsh (top left).

A *c.* late 1800s photograph of the Marsh family and friends. John Marsh Jr. poses here with his wife, Margaret Meyer Marsh, and their children: Josephine, Mae, and Edith. Also included in this photograph are Lydia Irene Hueston (their cousin) and Josephine van Natta (a friend).

John Marsh Jr., the son of John and Hannah Garlinghouse Marsh, was the father of Josephine Marsh Hollingsworth, Edith Marsh Zabrinske, and Mae Marsh Pope.

Henry Shenck at the Marsh's, *c.* 1900. Mr. Shenck worked for the Marsh family.

An earlier photograph of Henry Shenck, *c*. 1890.

Emma Kingston with Henry B. Marsh, *c*. 1900.

Ernest Marsh appears in the upper right corner of this photograph. The other two men in the photograph were not identified.

Harold J. Marsh, *c*. 1910.

The pond at John Marsh's estate in Scotch Plains. Careful inspection reveals two people on the opposite shore. The pond no longer exists.

The Marsh home after the blizzard of 1888. This is the side gate on Park Avenue.

A view of the corner of Park Avenue and Front Street after the blizzard of 1888. Notice the Stage House Inn across Front Street. Also notice the sign pointing to Plainfield.

A horse and carriage belonging to the Marsh family. These winter scenes of the Marsh estate were taken by Flora Garlinghouse Lacey, the niece of Mrs. Marsh.

An 1897 photograph of Flora Garlinghouse, the amateur photographer.

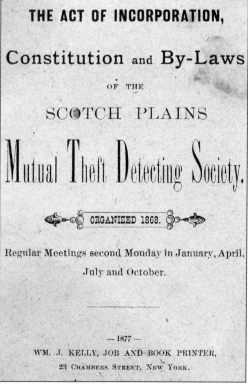

THE ACT OF INCORPORATION,

Constitution and By-Laws

OF THE

SCOTCH PLAINS

Mutual Theft Detecting Society.

◆◆ ORGANIZED 1868. ◆◆

Regular Meetings second Monday in January, April, July and October.

— 1877 —

WM. J. KELLY, JOB AND BOOK PRINTER,
23 CHAMBERS STREET, NEW YORK.

The "Constitution and By-laws" of the Mutual Theft Detecting Society. "This society has been chartered to protect of its members from theft." The initiation fee was $5, and yearly dues were $1. Members of this society were the more prominent and influential citizens of Scotch Plains; for instance, George Kyte, Thomas Young, the Coles, the Osborns, the Stanburys, the Hollingsworths, the Johnsons, the McKeuns, the Frazees, and the Ackermans were all listed in this pamphlet.

PROTECTION.

The Scotch Plains Mutual

Theft Detecting Society

INCORPORATED BY AN ACT OF THE LEGISLATURE OF N. J.

Article 3rd of said Act is as follows :—And be it enacted, "That every Member of said Society shall be empowered to arrest any person or persons whom they may find stealing, or in whose possession stolen property may be found, and bring them before a Magistrate to be dealt with according to law."

THE MEMBERS OF THIS SOCIETY, OF WHICH THE FOLLOWING IS A PARTIAL LIST

Joseph Clark,
Wm. C. Stanbury,
James C. Lyon,
Joseph M. Osborn,
Wm. H. Brower,
George R. Nicholl,
James A. Baker,

O. M. Putnam,
Loftus Hollinsworth,
John Robinson,
Lewis H. K. Smalley,
John L. Spencer,
Randolph Drake,
John Roselle,

Lewis Craig, M. D.,
George Miller,
A. D. Shepard,
R. B. Duyckinck,
Wallace Vail,
Frank Wiley.

W. E. Langley,
Francis E. Morse,
Bennit Brittin,
Theodore J. Ackerman,
James C. Freeman,
Lewis W. Miller, Jr.

HAVE ORGANIZED THEMSELVES INTO A

"PERPETUAL VIGILANCE COMMITTEE,"

Whose duty it is to be always on the alert, ever in readiness to go at a moment's warning in all directions in the pursuit, and will spare no pains to recover the property of its Members, and to arrest and inflict upon the guilty, summary and condign punishment.

By Order of the Society,

Dr. JOS. CLARK, Pres.

O. M. PUTNAM, Sec.

The Scotch Plains Mutual Theft Detecting Society, c. 1868. Incorporated by an act of the legislature of New Jersey, this was our "first neighborhood watch group."

Levi Darby, who participated in the Mutual Theft Detecting Society, was the Chairman of the Township Committee in 1878.

Joseph Osborn was one of the charter members of the Mutual Theft Detecting Society, c. 1870s.

A *c*. 1900 photograph of a Scotch Plains baseball team. George Vanderbilt is on the right side in the front row; Charles Heller is in the center in the back. (These identifications were listed on the back of the photograph.)

Another photograph of the same team with the bat boy. Notice the slight variations in the uniform shirts.

A Scotch Plains baseball team, c. 1900. The insignia "SP" on the uniform shirts denotes Scotch Plains. This was probably a semi-professional team from around the turn of the century, when baseball became popular in this country.

Local citizens gather at George Johnson's home.

Six
Schools

A c. 1905 photograph of School One. The first new public school building was constructed on Park Avenue in the 1890s at a cost of $18,000. It was designed by Stanford White as an adaption of Romanesque architecture. The building was originally opened as an elementary school, but within a decade it served as a high school as well. In 1926 it again reverted to being an elementary school, and it served in this capacity until its closing in 1974. Although it was in the National Register of Historic Buildings, the school no longer stands. A plaque now commemorates its site as a small testimonial to the great influence the building had on the many generations of students who passed through its corridors for over eighty years.

The students and teachers of School One, *c.* 1900.

A later view of School One. Notice the ivy on the building and the height of the trees.

These photographs chronicle some of the many festivities at School One.

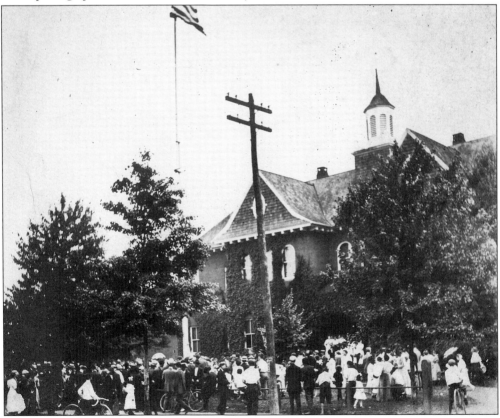

School One's Class of 1911. The students identified on the back of this photograph include Fred Coombs, Lloyd Seabolt, Evelyn Buckley, Margert Jalen, Marion Clark, Sadie Manning, Southard Oulivater, Nettie Ford, Grace Milick, Ruth Dunan, George Clark, Clifford French, Mary Murry, Rose Florence, and Sidney Lidgate.

The first grade class of School One in 1911. The teacher is Miss Bennette. The students, as identified on the back of the photograph, are, from left to right: (front row) Yarrious, Sabatino, R. Santosalvo, Mooney, Meyer, Meyer, Carrona, Myer, and Bopp; (second row) R. Prethee, Howith, E. Tramontano, unknown, and R. Williams; (third row) Santosalvo, Cristerfer, Peck, and Vrinive; (back row) Vrinive, unknown, DiDenoto, Tramontano, Conway, Wallpoll, and Orr. (It should be noted that the information on the back of the photograph was incomplete. Perhaps the author had forgotten many of the children's names.)

The eighth grade class of School One in 1912 consisted of: (front row) Margaret van Husen, Mildred Brahe, and Marion Clark; (back row) Walter Dermont, Anna Littel, John Southard, Sydney Lidgate, Pat Murray, John Horrack, and Wright McAnery. The unidentified person in the front row is probably the original owner of this photograph.

A c. 1900s photograph of an elementary school class of School One.

A postcard of elementary school students at School One.

Another view of School One created into a postcard.

An elementary school class at School One, *c.* 1900. Compare this interior shot, with the windows covered to prevent sunlight from washing out the photograph, to the one below.

A c. 1900 photograph of a classroom at School One. It appears as if the children's names are written on the blackboard to the left in the photograph.

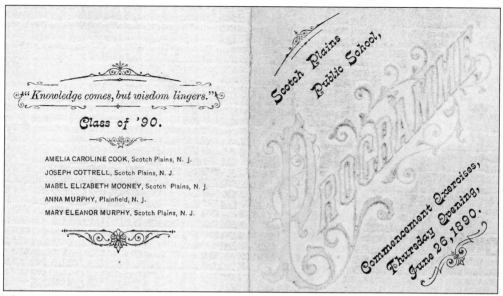

The Scotch Plains Public School Commencement Exercises Programme for 1890. Five students are listed on the "programme," which took place on Thursday evening, June 26, 1890, and included a performance from each student.

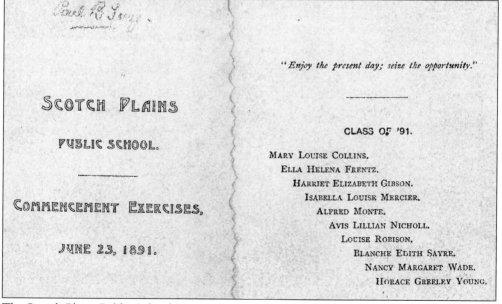

The Scotch Plains Public School Commencement Exercises Programme for June 23, 1891. The children's names are listed on the right.

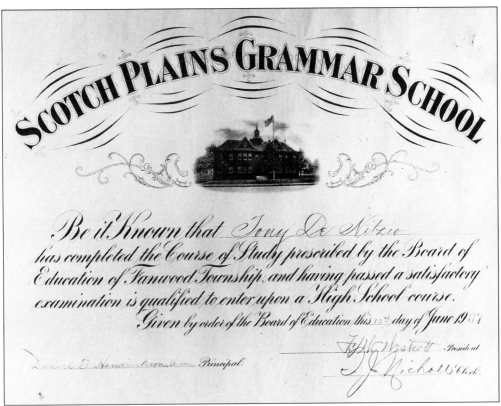

A Scotch Plains Grammar School Diploma from 1907.

The Willow Grove School, or School Two. This two-room wooden building was located near Lambert's mills. It served some Westfield residents, since District 11 included some sections of that town. The building was also used as a Sunday school.

School Three was located on Jerusalem Road in Scotch Plains. This building is currently being brought back into educational service.

School Four in Fanwood, c. 1926. This building is currently being used as part of the Children's Specialized Hospital.

Teachers at School Four in 1926.

Scotch Plains High School, located on Park Avenue in Scotch Plains, came into service in 1926. Today the building houses Park Middle School, for grades six, seven, and eight.

The seventh grade class of Scotch Plains High School in 1927. The teacher is Mrs. Hannah Stiglitz.

A later postcard view of Scotch Plains High School.

Seven

Churches

The Willow Grove Chapel on Raritan Road in Scotch Plains. In 1887, the cornerstone for this vine-covered stone building was laid. The building was completed in time for the Christmas service of 1888. The chapel still stands today, although many additions and renovations have been completed to accommodate the ever-growing congregation.

All Saints Episcopal Church on Park Avenue in Scotch Plains, *c.* 1950. The cornerstone for this building was laid on April 29, 1882, and the church opened for services on October 8 of the same year. A parish house, a portico, and new entrance are among the many additions to the building.

A postcard view of All Saints Episcopal Church.

The parish house of All Saints Episcopal Church on July 11, 1950.

The Fanwood Presbyterian Church, located at the corner of Martine and LeGrand Avenues in Fanwood. Construction for this building began in 1933. Previously, a survey had revealed that some Fanwood residents believed that they should have a church of their own. Services were held for a number of years in School Four until the church building was completed. By the time the first services were held in the new church, the congregation had grown to almost two hundred people. As the congregation grew, the building was modified by two additions.

The Church of Christ the Scientist on Midway Avenue in Fanwood. The building was purchased by the congregation from the State Highway Department and moved to its current site midway between Scotch Plains and Fanwood in November 1948. By the time the first service was held in the new church on December 19, 1948, the building had been completely renovated and redecorated by members of the congregation.

The First Methodist Episcopal Church on the corner of Forest Road and Mountain Avenue. The cornerstone was laid for this building on July 13, 1871, and the dedication ceremonies took place in February 1872. The building no longer stands.

Eight

Wartime and Beyond

Ira Gage Walker was the Scotch
Plains Township Committee
Chairman from 1907 through 1917.

This monument, located at the corner of Park Avenue and Front Street in Scotch Plains, was constructed by the Victory Celebration Committee of Scotch Plains to commemorate the contributions of our community to World War I. The captured German cannon was a gift from the government, in appreciation of the fact that Scotch Plains had the largest percentage of over-subscription to the Victory Liberty Loan in any non-banking community in the Second Federal Reserve District. This subscription tallied to almost $700,000. In a newspaper clipping located in the time capsule unearthed in the monument in 1995, it is stated that the monument is to serve as a "proper memorial to the boys who responded to the call of the Great World War, and the part which Scotch Plains took in the Victory Liberty Loan when the town raised $700,000 against its quota of $25,500. In doing so, the town won first prize, a captured German cannon . . . A ceremony was held to dedicate the monument and the honorable Jowett Shouse, Assistant Secretary of the United States Treasury, was orator of the day." This monument consists of an 80-foot steel flagpole, "an isle of safety to protect pedestrians, and at the base of the flagpole is a concrete pedestal upon which will be a bronze tablet showing the names of the 88 boys and one girl who responded to the call, three of whom paid the supreme sacrifice." The monument stands today, although it now commemorates all of our country's wars. It is currently being restored by the World War II Commemorative Committee.

The captured German cannon on the isle of safety at the monument.

The Daughters of the American Revolution marker at the monument, "marking the route through Scotch Plains of the Swift Sure Stage Line, Philadelphia to New York."

The celebration of Scotch Plains Week after World War I. Edward Ward and his family lived in this home, which is decorated for the celebration.

A photograph of the wives, mothers, and sisters of World War II servicemen from Scotch Plains. Although the list is incomplete, the following people are identified on the back of the photograph: (front row) Mrs. Carmen Meyer (Fred), Mrs. John Long, unknown, Mrs. Peterson, unknown, Mrs. Malek, unknown, Mrs. Fette, unknown, unknown, Mrs. Vernon, Mrs. M. DiFrancesco (Rose Santa Salvo), Mrs. L. DiFrancesco (Faith Mancini), and unknown; (second row) unknown, Mrs. Florence Sharkey (Ed), Mrs. M. Meyer, unknown, Mrs. C. Sharkey, Mrs. Bardoff, Mrs. A. Caruso, Mrs. J. Del Nero, Mrs. Tripet, Mrs. Wallace, unknown, Mrs. Debbie, and unknown; (third row) Mrs. Chechio, Mrs. D'Addamio, Mrs. Fantini, Mrs. J. Santo Salvo Sr., unknown, Mrs. Clare Fritz, Mrs. Huldabraun, Mrs. J. Prettie, Mrs. Peter Beck, Mrs. Levine, Mrs. Emery, and unknown; (back row) unknown, unknown, Mrs. C. Beck, Betty Mann, Brehm (Walter), unknown, unknown, Mrs. Prettie, Mrs. Art Runyon, and Mrs. Rau.

A sign of development in Scotch Plains off Park Avenue. The 1950s brought massive development to our towns. This sign attracted purchasers, especially veterans, to the growing community.

These newly-completed Cape Cod homes are of the standard bungalow design. They are still popular in Scotch Plains today.

An aerial view of the homes surrounding the St. Bartholomew the Apostle Church and School at 2032 Westfield Avenue in Scotch Plains. This view shows the Cape Cod homes of the 1950s, with the more recent split and bi-level homes at the top of the photograph. (Photograph courtesy of the Very Reverend Peter Zaccardo and St. Bartholomew's Roman Catholic Church)